BOOKS BY B. ELWIN SHERMAN

"Dear Witbones" --- Ask A Humorist!

The Miradors – Descensions of A Man

George W. Bush – On The Trips of His Tongue – A Linguistic Legacy

HumorUs (With the NetWits)

Toolkit In Paradise – The Self-Helpless Guide To A Decade of American Wit & Wisdom

Caught In The Shower Without A Pencil

Opening Closures – A Young Mother's Dying Declarations

Walk Tall and Carry A Big Watering Can

In Watermelon Salt – The Lost Richard Brautigan

THE DIOECIANS

THE DIOECIANS

His and Her Love

by

B. Elwin Sherman

Curry Burn Press ψ New Hampshire

© 2017 by B. Elwin Sherman

All rights reserved. No part of this book may be reproduced, stored in a retrieval system or transmitted in any form or by any means without the prior written permission of the author, except by a reviewer who may quote brief passages in a review for print media or internet newspapers, magazines or journals.

ISBN-13: 978-0-9982494-4-5

Designed & composed in Bookman Old Style
at Curry Burn Press

Cover Art, photos and design by B. Elwin Sherman.
Field Research and additional photos
by D. Lillian Sherman.

Printed in the U.S.A.
First Paperback Edition

Published by:
Curry Burn Press
P.O. Box 300, Bethlehem, NH 03574
www.witbones.com

Dedicated to

ARRON WILSON
&
SPENCER CHAMBERLAIN

*Do you **have** to have
a reason for loving?*

----- Brigitte Bardot

CONTENTS

At The End Of Prologue 15

Dummy Anthem Echoes 17

Comparison Study 19

A Witness To Her Kitchen Hand 21

His Kaleidoscope Forest Aviary 23

A Question Of Reclusion 25

The Night Fight Vacancy 27

Her Facebook Pout 28

Profane Telemarketing Foreplay 30

Father's Day Formal Wear 32

The Ocean Redecorator's Commission 34

The Dawn Of Old Magic 36

A Song Of Lagomorpha 38

The First Instrumentals 41

The Adolescent Hidden River 42

Inside Other Birds 44

The Discounted Breakfast 47
The Future Of Nasal Warfare 48
Her Civilian Erotic Day Planner 50
His Religion Problem 52
Her Almost A Double Paraphilian Wood Shed Metaphor-Metaphor 54
Runaway Pond Matrimony 56
Prescriptions 58
Love And Death Of The Blue Ancestral Cat 60
The Glory Window 63
Bleats And Toodles 69
The Less Virtual Dream of Darwin Debate 72
Whatever You Do, Don't 73
She Married A Man With A Leaf Blower 76
Long Litigation Of The Mother Daughter 79
The Fall Of Sir Isaac's Autonomics 84
Forward Passing On The Side 86
The Dioecians 88
Past The Future Of A Present Christmas 90
Your Notes 95

DIOECIOUS:

Having the male and female reproductive organs in separate flowers on separate plants.

AT THE END OF PROLOGUE

If you insist:
They have a music collection. In it,
you hear the melodies of Brahms,
Doc Watson, Jon Hendricks,
Frank Zappa and Eddie Cleanhead Vinson.

They have bookshelves. On them,
you see the musings of S. J. Perelman,
The Bible, Dick Gregory, Captain Marvel
and Jack Seward.

(Who?)

Jack Seward.
He wrote:
"Hara-Kiri: Japanese Ritual Suicide."

(You insisted.)

They have minds. Through them,
you feel regret, anxiety, joy,

wonder, madness, aversion and vengeance.
Whatever you take away from here will be true.
They'll not quibble with you.
They are yours to love or dismember.

Always that slim and dangerous distinction
between the two.

DUMMY ANTHEM ECHOES

A sagging gazebo sits here at the water's edge,
where the drum and tuba band is playing
in a hot settling dusk of their first summer together.

The musicians are local mainstays,
all Classically-trained, if you consider
a homespun, baton-defying, boom-bang tune
Classical.

Mischievous straying semitones,
half-quarter reaching for,
but never quite landing upon,
the elusive, errant upbeats.

The discordant concert of emerging love.

If not for these chugging replays,
this memory of their beginning
would die crumpled in a stuffy attic trunk
like the missed destiny of a tossed ventriloquist doll.

Across the lake in hazy affirmation
(no, *resignation* is better),
disappearing mountains throw their voices.

The well-tuned lovers sit like a chord
(no, *an arpeggio* is better),
embracing on their brassy shore,
rehearsing the strains of intemperate love songs
not yet written.

COMPARISON STUDY

How else could she say it with appropriate fuego?
Until their passions met, she'd never loved
and laughed so hard, so soft,
or felt so adored and amused.

But, yesterday he asked her:
"Do you love raisins as much as I do?"
That sent her into an existential tailspin,
wondering again if she could ever again
know another man's love without comparing it
to what she'd put into and taken out of her affairs
with others.

She must allow it instead to float free,
without judgment. The quiet and gentle,
the passionate and sensual,
the tough and gnarly, the fun and exuberant.
That's how she answered him.

But, today he hits her with another one:
"Is it hot in here, or is it me?"

"It's you," she snaps at him,
sick of all his endless introspection,
and it isn't well-received.
Not the answer he wanted.

He wanted a flopsweat camaraderie.

She calls to him from the ironing room,
putting it back on his readers:
"Do THEY love raisins as much as you do?"

From his home office, he can only hope
that you love poems ending with grapes.

A WITNESS TO HER KITCHEN HAND

As a short-eyed outsider anatomist, you see it,
even with an extra between blinks to really look,
as only a hand busied in menial necessity.

It's just a hand, you say, piteously.

So, he pities you, because you'll never know how
her flexing, flicking clump of saddle joint and
opposing fingers works his miracles.

Yes, you watch it nudge and knife chicken parts
onto a sideboard. Yes, it is so well-practiced
at dressing animal carcasses, that you,
as casual or keen observer,
see only a butcher's helper.

Poor pitiful functionary.
How you must now envy him,
knowing that he is also held and guided by it,
softly wrapped in its delicate authority,
as he hovers and positions himself to enter her.

Then, as contradictions are wont to do,
her kitchen hand serves him up its deepest clutch
by letting go.

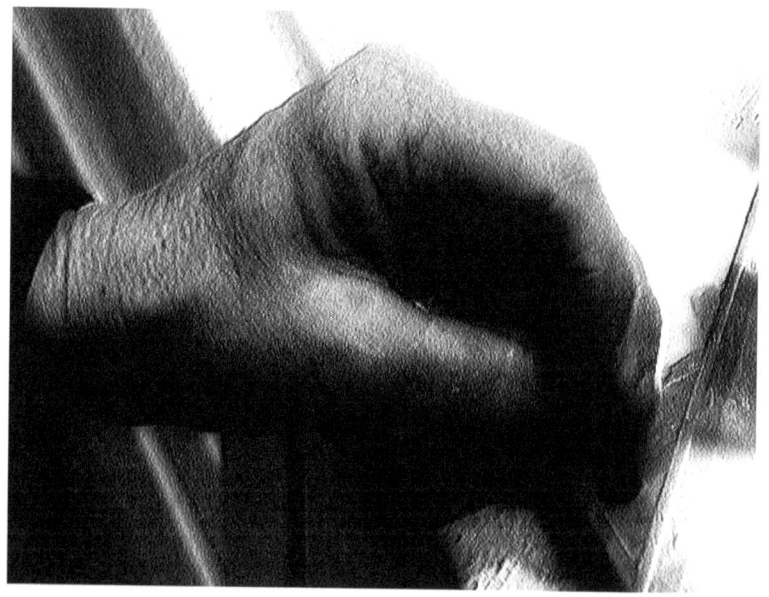

HIS KALEIDOSCOPE FOREST AVIARY

Before her, he didn't know:
1. He could choke his apple tree
with abandoned ice tongs.
2. Poplars are single parents.
3. Buckthorns are bullies.

Before her, how could he have known
that every day is arbor day,
when the refocused lens of love
turns from deciduous to evergreen.

Stunning, to not feel a wrong color in the bunch.
Are roots and limbs, flowers and weeds,
also that simple?
That incomprehensible?

Before her, he didn't know:
1. His hands in her hands hold all-season secrets.
2. Her hands in his hands are photosynthetic.
3. They live in the same light, air and water.

Last night they found the inevitability of seedlings there all this time, waiting like eggs.

This morning, every nesting bird in the world is the right color.

A QUESTION OF RECLUSION

She did have many friends.
In-the-body friendships, not
the cybernetic social network kind.
Those two-dimensional distancers.
(More on this later).

Why, then, had her life before him
gone on for months without a single phone call
or an invitation to do ... well ...
anything?

Why no sweet drop-ins
and impromptu glasses of iced teas on her deck?
She was fun and funny.
It was a nice deck.
She made good tea.

Was it because people saw her
as so settled and self-sufficient,
that she generally didn't come to mind
as someone who might enjoy going for a walk,

or munching on some BBQ
or licking an ice cream cone?
With another person, that is.

Solo, she enjoyed doing these things.
She had people tell her after-the-fact
(and for some it was a reiteration):
"Oh, I meant to invite you
to the gathering I had last week!"

Oh, really? A belated bullshit thank-you.
Liars.

Maybe it's because
she so rarely hosted anyone herself.
She worked too many hours for too many years,
and the precious free time was better spent

alone.

THE NIGHT FIGHT VACANCY

They have a tiff over nothing worth spending
more than a moment's labor
over.

As for her role in it, isn't it surprising
that a fleeting, poking-fun-at
and spooning into the backside
of the man she loves,
causes him to roll away from her fleshy mischief
and induce her insomnia?

The resulting wonderment
at her stupidity and self-flagellation
(NOT his rejection)
is more than plenty
to keep her staring at the ceiling all night,
saucer-eyed in the dark.

Come morning,
she hopes he'll still be there
to hear his version of things.

HER FACEBOOK POUT

She's his for the holding,
all warmed-up skin and cuddle,
but no, he'd rather connect
with those "like-minded people
with similar interests and talents."

Her loving arms are at the ready,
but no, he'd rather pour his sorrow
into mouse-clicking cyber-outliers
when it's HIS soul crackling with despair.

His depraved online multitude of "friends"
wants a public sounding board,
a scrolling camouflaged procession for all to see,
displaying their stained mortarboards of life
as if bleach were a virtue.

As if HE were their only seducing vice.

But, doesn't he know about this
seeming intimacy without commitment?

The kind that develops between
airplane seat mates and barstool neighbors,
strangers in one exaggeration,
confidantes in the next?

All of it vanishes
when the plane lands or bottoms go up.
"Nice talking with you! Have a nice day!"

Screw them. She hates Facebook.
Facebook is his giant coach compartment
in a suprasonic flying gizmo full of lying hijackers.

PROFANE TELEMARKETING FOREPLAY

He has so mastered an unfrenetic tone
when leveling a telephonic tongue-lashing
at bogus widget salesmen
and run amok quality assurancers,
that she thinks it a gift of his nature.

Like his locked and loaded manhood.

She, on the other hand, must work hard
at suppressing her high-treble piercing rants
when SHE is rightfully ticked off.

"Your product is a pile of dinosaur droppings,"
he tells the hucksters in his special code.
Calmly, monotonically, maddeningly.

Meanwhile, back at her time-biding womanhood,
she knows that he considers it
a plush gift of HER nature,

but when he hands IT the phone,

it breaks loose and screams:

"Your Goddamned monkey shit doesn't work!"

As co-lovers calm or tempestuous,

this is why they'll never be ordinary.

FATHER'S DAY FORMAL WEAR

Let's reduce his scientific day to poetry:

He is so-celebrated and defined by it,
because he'd once injected fluid
into another human being.

No trick to that,
and not the purpose or motivation at the time
for doing it.

Let's enlarge his poetic day to science:

Fluid turns to a descendant solid:
a solid whose main ingredient is ascendant fluid.
Biochemical engineer with a new tie.

Come next Mother's Day,
he'll give her this poem.

THE OCEAN REDECORATOR'S COMMISSION

She lives in what he can't see and hold.

That's why

this sudden strap iron band across his belly.

It's why

this feathering in his chest.

If she was there---

if that was her sunning herself

on that outcropping of slippery rock,

as if it had materialized that morning

solely to hold up her supinations---

if that pendulum toe-dip

and those reaching breasts

and that sun-proffering face

were only hers---

then the sinking shreds in his center

would be 99 percent unbearable.

But, it isn't her.

And he is struck motionless

by the consuming one percent of an empty seawall,

blotted by the box-white shadow

of her low-lying portrait removed.

THE DAWN OF OLD MAGIC

The best time to summon up
forgiveness and tolerance
is before they come due.

This is an inside trick that older lovers learn
after too many sleights of hands
and levitated partners
fall out of their invisible sleeves
and off prop platforms.

The missed cues scatter stage hands
and ruin the acts.

"Never go to bed without a goodnight kiss,"
the old magician tells them now, finally revealing
how longevity in love is no illusion.

Everlasting love has no false bottoms, steel rods,
telescoping wands, hidden wires or silent pulleys.

She's learned that bones and body parts
don't dematerialize and walk through bricks.
He's learned that puppet heads and card hearts
don't metamorphose into flaming paper
and back again.

The real trick, the real magic
is how to exit upstage,
slipping behind the night curtain
in the perfect redirection of misdirection.

Come the morning spotlight,
a lifelong devotion has no need
for prestidigitating locksmiths.

A SONG OF LAGOMORPHA

She takes a different road home,
past, through and over failing thrift shops,
failed book stores, potholes,
and exempted railroad crossings.
It is unlike her, but she is trying
to feel more like him.

He loves poetry.

She is a scientist and fears speaking to him
scientifically, when his poetry would do.
She's afraid that he is bored by her.
She's afraid he'll leave her over it.
But, she persists. She can't help herself,
and she wants him to feel more like her.

She loves science.

Later, he seizes the opportunity

for the right resistance,

the right yielding, the right openness

and black humor formulae

for their pillow talk pre-penetration.

Yes, he is a poet,

but he knows how to treat a scientist in the sack.

In her work, she spends the day doctoring the

unfortunates who suffer from anosmia, sialorrhea

and hypophonia. She tells him this all hifalutin'

wordy at bedtime, scaring herself, despite herself.

He springs it back on her as they begin to snuggle:

"Then tell me, Doctor Squeeziepie,

about the drooling whisperers

who couldn't smell you coming today."

They make love

like a mad poet laureate's lab rabbits.

THE FIRST INSTRUMENTALS

Until their sex under the bandstand,
all conical bores and flaring bells,

no one

had ever blown a twelve-bar blues
on her soprano oboe.

Until she'd arched into him like that,
all greenstick tension and gutbucket shudders,

no one

had ever ivory-slapped Johann Sebastian Bach
on his honky-tonk rocket 88.

THE ADOLESCENT HIDDEN RIVER

He takes her to his secret river swimming hole,
where tannins have turned the gravel beds
into shimmering copper underlayments.
The way the rippling surface plays against them
reminds him of her hair tangled in his hands.

Her hair isn't copper-colored. It is pepper black.
It doesn't shimmer. It shades.
But, his descension is a ringer
for the wincing pleasure it gives her
at this first immersing.

Another perfection of differences
as they go into water together for the first time.

He's in it immediately.
A stiff stand, a knee-spring,
a full flailing leap, all abrupt,
committed and consuming.

She edges in.

Buckling hesitations, dipping herself

like a stiff sponge,

all incremental, posing, tentative

and slow saturating.

Oh … and the truth is:

even in her teens,

she was always terrified of teenagers.

INSIDE OTHER BIRDS

Somehow, she ruins the safety of his sleep cocoon.
She only wants to be let in to his deepest slumber.

She doesn't mean to peel away
the swaddling envelope, the sanctuary he finds
in adding more weight, more blanket layers,
piling up and wrapping himself in more of less
of the wakeful world.

Now he is lying naked, curled on his side,
shuddering and crying out, sleepless but not awake.
She holds his head, his hands, his body,
but it doesn't comfort him.
She re-places the covers over him.
That should help.
She doesn't know what else to do.

He explains that cocooning gave him peace
in those years of being alone,

and the loneliness of being with a comatose wife

who couldn't respond to him.

Well, damn him, if he is so over her,

over her and that terminal bedside vigil,

why does he still need this soft barricade?

Where and what is she?

Does he still feel alone with her?

Is she useless and vacant?

What is passion if not received by the beloved?

Wing bones are so much more

than the internal foundations of flight.

She loves him and doesn't want to feel alone, either.

HIS DISCOUNTED BREAKFAST

After the afterglow,

after she is up and gone off to her research lab,

he gets up and finds the note on their kitchen table:

> *Good morning my sweet dawn surprise lover. (You were delicious!) Today in the real estate listings, I found this:*
>
> `Look! Look! Look! A bargain at any price! Views into perpetuity!`
>
> *This morning I feel like life with you is priceless property. I feel perpetual, because life without you would have a price tag, and that would be ... ME!*
>
> *See! See! See! There's cooked bacon in the fridge, burned just the way you like it!*

Aha! Some of his poetic appetite

is transferable after all,

and he doesn't mind cleaning the plate,

chipping at the sticky yolk, mindful of her cooking,

knowing that she'd eaten the last of the eggs

just the way he doesn't like them.

THE FUTURE OF NASAL WARFARE

(Zeitgeber [pronounced "sight-gey-ber"].
Definition: An external cue.)

There are nights when he wants to begin the day
with the sunset of his dark poetry.
There are days when she wants to end the night
with the sunrise of her shining science.

They don't have to tell you
how this can foul up the circadian harmony
of their composite life. They compromise
by melding zeitgebers:

If he silently looks, she will listen to him.
If she stares incredulously, he will touch her.

Neither has decided
(and it's early enough that the question
has not yet been posed)

what the other will do

when either of them,

without warning or reservation,

farts in bed.

HER CIVILIAN EROTIC DAY PLANNER

Lest he think her deranged,

she points out that today

she purchased for him the remaining two pairs

of (unworn, tags intact) black jeans

from the Windfall Consignment Shop.

She also had a delicious maple walnut cone

jimmied over melted chocolate,

downtown at the Whippi Dip.

Proof positive that she is doing A-OK.

In other domestic news, the electricians are coming.

Tomorrow they will have wires

connecting their living room ceiling fan

and it's a fucking finally miracle.

All these years a quixotic joke,

dangling up there mocking them,

all idle and evil and dumb dust dead-decorative.

Sensing the time and room
for a techno-pop seduction, she posits:
If they have no specific plans on Sunday,
could they visit the hardware store?

They could buy automatic garage door openers,
louvered vents and floodlamps.
They could use his big deal
10 percent military discount.

Then, howzaboutit, toots,
we could cool it hot and ball ourselves silly
under an overhead finally fucking indoor breeze?

His call.

HIS RELIGION PROBLEM

She was just pulling out of her sleep this morning
as he was pulling into another town.
It was another soft foggy morning on the deck
and she wondered if there had been auroras
above last night's clouds.

Rats.
Too much contemplation, too late.

Funny fellow riders on the mass transport today,
both to and from Boston on the T.
A large pregnant woman on the bus,
both directions,
blankly watching the reruns of insipid sitcoms,
her husband dozing in another decade.

But, when the weepy with-childer
smacked her impregnator awake on the return trip
and announced with far too much parturient fuss,

that her favorite "Friends" character

had just kissed his grandmother,

thinking she was dead

when she was alive?

She twice drops her phone

through all the theatrics.

He once retrieves it.

HER ALMOST A DOUBLE PARAPHILIAN WOOD SHED METAPHOR-METAPHOR

Yes, she had built the wood shed herself
and she loved-loved it, but there was nothing
unnatural about it. She just loved-loved it
the way one love-loves accidental beauty.

Yes, the exterior wood strappings were inadequate
and peeling away, and yes, he was right-right:
woodscrews would've been better.
But, he was right-right about so many other things
that she wouldn't yield to him on this.
She loved-loved and accepted the failing nailings
unconditionally.

Yes, those backside rotting wood panels did allow
undershed access to small animals
without them hole-tunneling their ways in.
Squirrels? Chipmunks? Fine with her. Welcome!
Walk right in, skunks and woodchucks!

She accepted them, too.

Yes, the dog-leg rafters made perfect niches
for interior wasp infestations: the nasty white-faced
variety that stung without provocation.
Welcome, even you, wicked wasps!

There was one crumbling board on the ramp.
It compelled anyone to take an unnatural step
entering, and a perilous one leaving.

Alright. She could learn to hate-hate that.

RUNAWAY POND MATRIMONY

(*For the residents, then and now, of Glover, Vermont*)

As weddings went, they were professionals.
Each with prior connubials:
He'd had his:
two, ending in death and/or desertion.
She'd had hers:
one ending in The Green Mountain State,
one in Canada, not open for discussion.

Still, marriage was the only way out for them.

The justice of the peace told them:
"Take him? Take her? Hitched!"
were all the out-loud avowals
needed to legally bind wedding mates.
All the rest, except for the catering,
was pomp and circumstantial paper tradition.

Why not, then, have it all their way?

Pledging troths at the shallow top

of an infamous Vermont field,

once the 70-foot deep bottom of a pond.

History said it had been sucked dry that way

by overzealous 19th Century miller's helpers

attempting to divert only enough water

for his gristmill, when all the earth let go

and the damn fools drained the whole thing.

Forever.

What could be a more symbolic longevity launchpad?

A pledged covenant of eternal love,

standing in a place where

empty space

would never again be

no space.

PRESCRIPTIONS

She apologizes for the mythical and monstrous
nature of her worries about who she is
and who she is not to him. What if
they are plain and simply more straightforward?
Simple speak. Plain talk.

Can she just declare that no, she is as fragile
as spun glass, but ask him to hold her tight
for two seconds,
                one.................two..................
and she'll be okay?

Can he just declare that yes, she is as lustrous
as tumbled rocks, but ask her to let him go
for two seconds,
                two..................one..................
and he'll be okay?

If she can and he can, they will lose their fear.

Yes, that one. The worst one.

The fear that they've been busy

behind the scenes,

finding each other wanting

in some critical way or another.

Maybe now they are learning to say

what is right there,

true in crystalline timeframes.

One or the other or both.

Now, his head problem can be just a head problem,

sleeping on it and calling her in the morning,

and her aloneness can be just a woman alone

singling-in on her side of the bed, doubling up.

Applied as directed.

LOVE AND DEATH OF THE BLUE ANCESTRAL CAT

Down to the ground she went at the dump,
dropping the stupid Dufy blue cat
and tripping over it as she approached the blue bin,
arms laden with their week's other recyclables.

Did he mention that it was a broken art deco
heirloom Bakelite cat with jutting spiky claws,
designed to snag the dump-dallying shoestring
of a five-foot woman determined to save
a pre-terminal environment from itself?

In this world, it does lessen the insult
if a body is waylaid in the midst
of any altruistic performance,
but it doesn't make a doodly-squat difference
to the injury. Ankle & foot bones
couldn't care less about altruism.
Or neatness. Or glory. Or their designated missions.

She could have been pivoting

to chase a live clueless cat,

unschooled in traffic hazards,

one turn of the head away from road kill.

Or she might've been half-awake,

rising from the commode,

overreaching for her ultrasonic toothbrush,

when slip! snap!

There went the talus.

A 60-inch heroine to him either way, he holds

her bruised and conscience-less lower extremity

tonight in his nestling hands, like he is cradling

that near mortally wounded live cat,

and the always dead and toothless plastic one.

How she loves him. Loves him. Loves him.

THE GLORY WINDOW

She thought that the Service would be
a successful Catholic funeral mass,
but because she was neither Catholic nor believer,
she wouldn't be sure. Perfect. It didn't matter.
If anything went wrong,
she wouldn't know the difference.

It was her first funeral since she was a little girl,
when she was taken to her Grandmother's.
She remembered the day, still a favorite
after dinner table tale, thinking how odd
that Nana should sleep
when everyone else was talking about her.

After she'd approached the bier
and poked the stilled, waxy cheek---
"Wake up, Nana!" ---
her grandfather had fainted
and fallen into the open coffin.

Now, she was going to say a grownup goodbye
to a dead dear friend, and greet the survivors
in her own way.

She did appreciate the sing-alongs
led by a gifted soprano with an irritating vibrato.

She welcomed the sit-stand-kneel rotations,
limbering up for the Communion wafers,
wanting to taste them and the blood of Christ,
but she didn't.

She wasn't thirsty or hungry or willing enough

to play public impostor

and stir up a Eucharistic uproar.

And ... gluten-free? Her celiac disease?

That's enough said about that.

She felt especially sorry for the little waxy Jesus

pinned down on the Cross:

an uncomfortably dangling mini of a man.

The priest one-handedly thrust the model crucifix

heavenward, and with an emphasis

hollow as a church, pointed other-handedly

to her departed friend's boxed-in face.

Looking for all the other world

like a postage-due diorama, he shouted:

"From the day of this woman's birth,

she was marked with the sign of Jesus!"

An opportunistic auctioneer of everlasting death
at the scene of an unnatural disaster,
and no bidders. Hell, yes,
she was cynical, but it felt good.

He then placed the little Redeemer
on the closed half of the open casket,
It rested there, supine and suppressive
for an hour-long abdominal crunch.
Poor sweet plastic mini-Jesus
with the bloody six-pack abs.

Was it soul-juggling risky
to feel pity and disgust
when reverence was called for? She did.
And she didn't care.

Many mourners rubbed tears from their eyes
and blew their noses, but the tears were
crocodilian and the noses crackly dry.
Were they only thinking of the fallen woman's
mortality mocking theirs?

All was exposed when the priest aimed
and swung that smoking thurible directly (it seemed)
at her, exposing her as an agnostic interloper.
It puffed clouds of incense, wafting over
and igniting her mucosae, watering and juicing
up her eyes and nose with real tears
and genuine mucus.

Luckily, she thought, they were not deep into April
and the season of those stinking Easter lilies.
No doubt this eliciting agent of God
was hard-of-smelling and he would've ordered them
en masse, too.

She left surprised, confessing to herself that maybe
she could, going full against her godless grain,
become fond of Catholic perks:
the church ladies' after-Service spreads and pies.
The quilts and the jams and donated gamblings.

"There could be some redemption

in this Eternity biz, after all,"

she tells him late that night.

He pulls her closer to him like a shutter.

"BLEATS AND TOOTLES"

He was astonished by her oboe-playing prowess.
Astonished, because he thought
she'd used up all the surprises
she ever could or would spring on him,
by marrying him.

Before the nuptials, he hadn't known
she was an oboist. This confounded her, because
she'd written to him, months before the wedding,
quite specifically mentioning, if you please,
her oboeing.

She'd been so clear about it, recounting how
she would swoon whenever she opened
the small, cracked, black leather case,
and out came "the intoxicating smell
of cork, wax, wood, and what have you,
spittle?" Yes, he remembered.

But, he thought she was only romanticizing
about an old collectible, the way someone does
when they've found a vicarious means
of living in a previous life by holding on
to a treasured tangible of the dead.

The oboe case looked like it belonged
to a once extinct pediatrician,
found and lost and come around again
for one last home-visit dispensary.

She unfastened the cover and gently lifted
the components from their red velvet molds
like she was defusing a bomb.
Bell, upper and lower joints, staple, reeds.

She assembled the pieces, all the while telling him
how she used tucking, squeezing, drawstring
pressure: the double-lip embouchure
essential for mastering double reed woodwinds:

"My teeth and lips, my mouth corners, my tongue,

my stomach muscles --- everything works

with how you trap air, and how you release it.

It's all part mechanisms ... and part magic."

He'd never been so turned on by music metaphor.

Yes, including the 60's.

When she finally played, the uncollectible ghost

of Marcel Tabuteau leapt into the room,

a dead and intangible treasure, sprung

from the pages of a 1939 Time Magazine article.

It filled the air with her capture

of its "pure bleats and thrilling tootles."

Astonishing.

THE LESS VIRTUAL DREAM OF DARWIN DEBATE

Monkeys pick nits

from the heads of their mates.

Why shouldn't she trim his beard?

WHATEVER YOU DO, DON'T

(not dedicated to Garrison Keillor)

Honey, I'm begging you, whatever you do, don't,
if I have left this earth and he hasn't,
ever allow a prowling, recitation-throttling
Garrison Keillor, to come
within a literal stone's throw
or a figurative radio-play couplet
of my poetry.

His cramping Writer's Almanac narration
(wait for the perfect rhyme and meter)
is tepid, vapid, oral defecation.
ACK!

Mr. Keillor would sportscast my lines
in that stale, top-to-bottomheavy,
peaking and plunging basso profundo,
last gasping, grasping breathiness of his,
as if melodrama was a sealed tomb,

overflowing with wilted roses horseshoes,
and I was the interred also-ran nag.

His mumble-purring wavy ruse of phony phonic bliss
(wait again for the throaty, limerickitschy march),
would turn my soundless lettered muse
into an aural piss.
ACK! ACK!

I'm begging you, my love, if you love me
(assuming I die first, which we both believe I will),
please promise to never let my written immortal
afterglows ever be lit up by the threnodical,
inchworm-bleating, snuffled, come-alonged
extra-undulated, over-modulated,
out-loud winching wincings of Killer Keillor.

I don't care what they offer you
or how starving you are.
Don't.

Gary Edward Keillor can turn a bowl of honey

into a sagging sack of soggy powdered saccharin.
Please. Please. Please. Don't ever let my work
become a drenched bag
of his acoustic artificial sweetenings.

"Okay okay OKAY! Enough already! I promise!"
she interrupts my rant,
and with an evil eye glint,
naughty to the quick,
neutralizes me with his signature sign-off:

"if you'll promise to always be well,
do good work,
and keep in touch."

ACK!
ACK!
ACK!

SHE MARRIED A MAN WITH A LEAF BLOWER

When this was revealed, too late,
she thought that an annulment
might not be the worst way out.

What could be more foolish
(dismayed at the prospect of now spending her life
with a useless tool gadgeteer)
than a man blowing leaves around the yard
with one of those lazy, loud, futile, dumb,
embarrassing, eco-awful noisemakers?

He might as well be chasing himself
around the world.

Alright, alright. Yes, yes, yes. He made her laugh,
and he loved animals and babies and kites
and he knew exactly when,
and where, and just-right how
to lift and tip her eager rocking chair. Oh, God, yes!

But, a leaf blower? Was that reconcilable?
Yes, it was, after he told her that he leaves leaves
to Mother Nature's composting winter
and Her clean-up to a windy spring.

Don't worry. He's only ever used the thing
to blow-dry the Harley after a good wash,
or to blast out the garage dust.

Whoosh. What a relief then and again,
sitting behind him, riding the bitchbar
around the seasons.

To Hell with the fossil fuel
eco-hypocrisy.

She especially loves
the autumn foliage runs.

LONG LITIGATION OF THE MOTHER DAUGHTER

A long time since she'd visited her mother,
and holy cow there was Mum,
barely bent but even shorter, standing
half-in, half-out of the house,
just as she'd always lived.

If thresholding was a verb, she'd use it here.

For the first time, she saw the passings
and passages of the invincible days, weeks,
months and years for what they truly were:
more than nine decades of cruel pyrrhic victories
and illusions of timelessnesses.

For the first time, she felt it impossible
for her mother to ever look any older.
All the penultimacies of death were there:
sags, wrinkles, compressions, expansions,
discolorations, softenings, hardenings, tilts.

The only thing that could change now?

An absent heartbeat.
The stilled bellows of breath.
And those awful beach pants.

For the first time, she thought this visit with Mum
might be their last one together.
She thought this until the old woman spoke
at dinner, and the first spunky disorder of business
was? You guessed it: she'd picked the wrong wine.

Ever the errant and untimely first-born daughter,
she again hadn't disappointed,
by the act of disappointing.

She'd retrieved and poured the wrong sweet white:
"The Scuppernong, not the Carlos!"
Mum admonished, dismissing daughter, wine,
and lifetimes of learned curves
with the back of her waving hand.

Then, as if her dismissal wasn't dismissive enough,
she scrunched up that up that nonagenarian nose
and added the injury's insult:
"That is the DINNER wine,
  not the COCKTAIL HOUR wine!"

For the first time, as dutiful daughter,
she moved unknowingly into the distinction
between caregiving and caretaking.

She fetched the wrong snacks.
No, those were the KALE chips.
No, those were the BAGEL chips.
No, those were the OTHER bagel chips.
Yes, those! The SNACK chips!
Each of these failed missions meant
another trip to the kitchen.

Mum's mental dissonance was now the string
difference between piano and violin,
where C-sharp is not D-flat.

Easier to "Just Do the Carol Merrill act,"
one sister had warned prior to her visit,
"and keep looking behind Door Number Three.
It's a different prize every time you open it."

Life with a pre-terminal mother
was now familial game-show inside jokes:
canned sets of strategies designed to distract,
fill the gaps, and control. Some luckily, some blindly,
and some, yes, avengingly.

She was nearly deaf herself, trying to be heard
over Mum's blasting TV, tuned-in to watch a
"handsome Henry" Connick Junior concert.
Later, in Judge Judy's courtroom, she got to
the final metaphor and best symbiosis of this poem:

The closed captioning was activated,
but Mum couldn't keep up.
Someone needed to show the CC guys
how plaintiffs and defendants
will sometimes sit in the same dock.

THE FALL OF SIR ISAAC'S AUTONOMICS

Today, they are not like skydivers freefalling
in terminal velocity. Up there, at that speed,
slow is fast. Make a move, and zip!
The results are precipitate and Newtonian.

Change the angle edge of a hand, tuck the knees,
arch the back, and your body immediately
changes direction, speed and attitude,
snapping-to it in the blasts of winds.

Then comes the unforgiving rule of
speedy air descent: "The body follows the head."
Up there, if you look that way,
you will go that way.

And, up there?
It had better be where you wanted to go.

But, down here,

after arguing all morning about the car,

he realized it was the head following the body.

Down here, Newton came up short on one law:

"Any moving body ...

disputing another body at rest and at length,

should change his mind and buy the other car,

to suit the color and cargo space preferences

of his equal and opposite partner,

assuming he wants to keep the balance

of their accelerated mass

... in motion."

FORWARD PASSING ON THE SIDE

In her mind, the great mysteries of life
were not the pyramid's architects,
or its builders,
or how trees communicate,
or the lifespans of certain sharks.

As a scientist, she was comfy with theories,
hypotheses and probabilities.

For her, it could be, and most likely is or was,
ancient extraterrestrial triangulators,
subterranean fungal kinships,
and vertebral rings.

In his mind, the great truths of life
were not lost love's longings,
or its unrequited ghosts,
or how human scents seduce,
or the broken promises of post-graduate boyhood.

As a poet, he was comfy with walkaway love,

the urgency of smells,

and photo booth sex.

For him, it could be,

and most likely is or was,

imagined unkept rendezvous,

seasonal mating pheromones,

and loverboy quarterback

heartthrob spoilers.

THE DIOECIANS

She ever the scientist.
The first time they exposed themselves
by bringing out the old photos, she chose
one of herself on a horse: "in my cowgirl phase,"
taken the summer she'd offset her college dues
by driving a chuck wagon.

Yes, he'd heard her right:
Chuck wagon driver.
At Yellowstone, cooking
for tenderfooting tourists.
Yes, a real old-timey wagon.
Real horses. Real campfires.

The only job she'd ever trained so little for.
Before or since.
"They just handed me the reins, the grub,
and told me to follow the horses."
Very unscientific. And, she'd loved it.

He ever the poet.

Would she think him a savage?

A marching contradiction

in this barracks photo.

Some sneer, some sadness,

some madness,

all undying youth.

Yes, she'd heard him right:

Marine.

In the world, taking & giving orders

from superiors, to subordinates, for himself.

Yes, a real stiff-backed Jarhead.

Real bullets. Real gutturals.

The only job he'd ever trained so much for.

Before or since.

"They just handed me the rifle, the men,

and told me to follow the history."

Very un-poetic. And, he'd loved it.

PAST THE FUTURE OF A PRESENT CHRISTMAS

You want me to do what, m'dear?
Stand under the mistletoe?
You do know that its sap is toxic?
You are aware that its haustorium
punctures and draws the lifeblood
from its host plant?

You must know that it's a parasite?
It has separate male and female flowers.
A true Dioecian.

Aha! That's why you're doing this to me.
For your lovely little silly book.

"Just come plant yourself under here,
my festive floral beauty,
and lock up some juicy holiday lip with me.
We'll work on the blooms later."

B. ELWIN SHERMAN holds Nursing and Theater Arts degrees from North Shore Community College and Franconia College. He attended Chautauqua School of Music, leading to his membership in the Piano Technicians' Guild and a stint in assuming the family business in piano tuning & regulation after his father's passing. He's written nine books, and is a Senior Wire News Service syndicated humor columnist. He's a member of the National Society of Newspaper Columnists and recipient of a Robert Benchley Society Award for Humor. His passion for the pianoforte, creative writing, and the great indoors is balanced by his love of both the indisputable and the always contested.

D. Lillian Sherman might sometimes take some exception to some of this.

D. LILLIAN SHERMAN holds a BSc in Biochemistry from McGill University and a PhD in Biology from Yale University. She completed a postdoctoral research fellowship at the University of Wisconsin-Madison. She spent decades in academic labs participating in basic research programs. Some projects were subsequently applied to practical applications and others still show promise, but the goal was always modest: to add a splash of information to the oceans of knowledge. Her passion for science, mathematics, and the great outdoors is balanced by her love of well-crafted fiction, poetry, musical performance, and capturing observations on a sketchpad.

B. Elwin Sherman does not always fully appreciate this about her without cues.

YOUR NOTES